TALES OF MATILDA THE ROBIN

Matilda Is Missing

Jennifer Skyers

A new family had joined the nestling area down by Lake Wentworth in Rochester. It was the Rochester Robin family. They had moved into the area to start afresh after losing all but two of their fledglings to Mr Crow.

Winter had been harsh, very, and from the neighbouring robin families which also shared the nestling area, many had sadly become malnourished from the lack of food, whilst others had become food for the scavenging crows who could often be seen lurking around the area.

The crow was seen as the arch enemy, showing no mercy to anything that they wished for to satisfy their hunger for tasty foods.

Mr Crow particularly had a penchant for young robins and had been known to ransack and intrude on the robin families who were busy looking after their young fledglings. Some of the young robin families felt the need to install someone to help protect them. This was in the form of Mr Starling who had quite a sharp beak and who would defend his friend the robins if the crows even attempted to come near where the robins nestled.

The starlings had a distinctive yellow beak and could easily camouflage with the surrounding foliage, a Godsend for the menacing crow. The starlings also had an excellent mimic and with their loud screech, which could be as loud as the screech for a car coming to a sharp halt, would deter even the most obstinate intruder. However, the greatest benefit of having the starlings as their security support is that the starlings had the added advantage of being able to swivel their eyes backwards, affording them the ability to watch out for any impending danger that may be approaching without even lifting their heads! A perfect deterrent from any potential intruder and that of any crow.

The Rochester Robin family owed their life to the brave intervention of the starling family. Their first brood had almost been eaten by crows, but the starlings had intervened and stopped the scavenging crows from obliterating the entire family.

Mummy Robin was due to give birth soon and it had been a long night, but finally the fledglings were delivered. She had given birth to four babies who were huddled together to stay warm inside the nest. Mummy just wanted to rest.

Their hatchlings were not much to look at, as they had yet to bloom and earn their distinctive red plumage which notably would be the envy of their neighbours. In the meantime, they had to be content with their oh so slightly transparent yellowish plumage and brown feathering.

It was customary for the female to brood over the nestlings for a week while the male robin went hunting for food for the entire family. After the first week, both parents would take it in turns to hunt for food to feed the chicks until they left the nest at the end of the second week. Meanwhile, the babies were maturing, and they would be almost fully feathered by the tenth day.

It had not only been a busy time for the Rochester Robin family, but the area was expanding with fledglings of other bird species. Families were being born daily and the area was expanding, awash with baby starlings, the cutest blue tits, the songster thrushes, sparrows, and hummingbirds.

Soon the robins would be seen standing aloft from the other fledglings as they paraded their bright red plumage for all who would care to notice. Soon they would become all furry with their feathers providing a coat which would offer much protection, comfort, and warmth. In the meantime, Mummy Robin had the all-important job of spreading the warmth of her fully adult body over the fledglings.

Morning had broken and the ground was still wet from the dew. However, the sun was breaking through offering hope of a brighter warmer day as the gentle breeze rustled through the limp branches. Back at the Rochester Robin's nestling and nestled amongst the trees was Daddy Robin, his beak dribbling with the dew which had fallen that spring morning. Peering through the wet leaves, he hopped forward surveying the environment wondering what he could provide for the morning menu. This is what Daddy Robin did every day to provide for his growing brood.

Daddy Robin dug away at the shrubbery which concealed the entrance to their nest. Daddy Robin was preparing to exit the warm cosy surroundings of the nest on a mission minded into creating a tasty menu for his beloved family.

Gathering food for his brood was something which Daddy Robin took pride in. He was instinctive as a parent and often he would gather food for his camp mates, like Daisy the blackbird, Kitty the song thrush, and Willow the warbler.

The nestling site for the birds was very close to a rural area where a young woman lived. Her name was Margaret Bindle. She was a little over thirty and lived alone most of the time as her husband had taken employment in the USA. Some of the locals had referred to her as a little bohemian with her hair held back in a tight bun and her choice of attire which harked back to a bygone era - the 1950's, with cinched in waistlines, military inspired wide shoulders tea party dresses and saddle shoes. She was certainly well kept, but not a follower of fashion.

All the birds from the nestling area adjacent to her home were enamoured with Ms Bindle as her garden was an open enclave to birds of every species, from song thrushes to swallows, as she would place food on a feeder so that they could help themselves.

Her garden was a hive of an assortment of odd bits and bobs including obsolete kitchenware such as cast-iron kettles, wicker hanging baskets, old boots, even an old tin bath.

Ms Bindle's quirkiness and eccentricity had no limitations. Chaotic, a hoarder and holding on to the dying emblems of a bygone era, she would leave food for the birds in all kinds of unlikely locations, in the shed, hidden away in kettles, old boots which had been thrown out or discarded, hanging baskets which graced the front elevation of the conservatory and even in the pockets of old army coats which were hanging in the shed which she would often be seen wearing when doing the garden or planting. Picture the scene!

The weekend had arrived sooner than expected, almost six days from the day the robin babies were born. Soon they would be fully grown, sporting their familiar red plumage and ready to leave the nest and gain their own independence.

It was a wet grey Sunday morning which greeted the robin family. Meanwhile a little earlier, Daddy Robin had taken his early morning flight to gather food, but to the family, especially Matilda, it appeared that he had been a long time gone. Hence Matilda, emboldened by her own self-confidence, had grown restless and decided to venture out to find food and maybe join Daddy Robin in his search.

She had woken up feeling a little more hungry than usual as Daddy had not brought home as much food as he had done on other days. She darted a quick look at Mummy who was attending to her siblings, fluttered her tiny wings and took aim for the skies. Gliding along through the air at minimal speed, Matilda surveyed the world around her. She spied Jemima the song thrush darting across the lawns below scurrying after a worm. They had met yesterday when both families were introduced.

"Well, she will not go hungry," Matilda thought to herself. "I just must find food for our family," Mummy would be so proud.

Matilda navigated her way off the branches and finally perched on the windowsill of a house which happened to be Margaret' Bindle's house. Peering through the window of the conservatory, she spied a round of bread cut into tiny, neat squares. "They look yummy," she chirped and tapped her beak on the window looking for a way to gain entrance to access the food which looked so appetisingly sumptuous.

Matilda couldn't find a way in even though Ms Bindle usually left the window open to the conservatory. She circled the house a few times flapping her wings frustratingly as she tried to find an open window. Unperturbed, Matilda continued flying around the back of the house looking for a way in. However, it seems on this occasion that Ms Bindle had forgotten to leave a window open in the conservatory for her bird friends. Disappointed, Matilda flew around about four houses down the block and spied a couple sitting outside having lunch. "They look friendly," she thought and wondered if they would like to share their lunch with her. She was oh so hungry. Matilda circled around where the table was spread and flew in close. She perched herself on the edge of the table and busied herself surveying the food. In the meantime, the couple had popped back into the house to bring out the rest of the food.

The table was set for a king, or so it looked like it was. The finest bone China tea set was on display. The pattern on the tea set was decorated in a blue painting of peacocks and edged in gold paint. Sandwiches were cut neatly with the edges removed.

There were also finger donuts filled with cream and finished off with a caramel topping. There was also a cream sponge cake However, Matilda's eyes were drawn to the arrangement displayed to the left of the table. There were several bowls of cherries, berries, grapes, and an assortment of nuts. Some of the spread looked very much familiar like what Daddy Robin brought home after his journey to hunt for food. Had Matilda struck gold?

A telephone could be heard in the hallway and the doorbell chiming as the guests arrived and excitable chatter as the couple returned to the garden with the rest of the lunch and their guests. Matilda preened herself to perfection, hoping to obtain a last-minute invite to the sumptuous lunch. But she soon learned that she was not welcome and would not be going away with any food. "Shoo, shoo, you dirty rascal," the smart lady said. "We do not have room for you at our table. Out of here, you are not welcome here," the woman continued. Slowly unfolding her wings, Matilda reluctantly flew out of the garden and soared to the top of a tree looking down at the tea party that was about to commence, wishing somehow that she could have sampled just a little of the food on offer.

A little forlorn at such a sharp rebuke and being denied a seat at the table, Matilda hoped to find her luck elsewhere. She perched herself on the top branches of the willow tree and surveyed the other gardens around her. From where she was positioned, she could see another garden which had a bird table in the centre of it. Her eyes lit up, excited at the prospect of finding food to take back home. She swooped down to the table but soon became downcast as she realised that someone had got there before she did. Nevertheless, she poked around at the food remaining on the table hoping to salvage enough to take back to her nest. As she did so, Matilda became nervous as she was startled by an object which swiftly darted past her, unsure as to whether she had seen a bird of prey or perhaps a fox! Matilda composed herself and went back to the task in hand of gathering the remains of the food left on the table. This will not be enough to feed a family of six she thought. Nevertheless, she continued poking around the bird table and then out of the corner of her eye, she spied the thing which she had seen moments earlier dart past her again. She had not been dreaming, it was a fox! She froze on the spot as she peered at the fox. Although Matilda was very frightened, she too was oh so inquisitive.

Matilda had been told about the dangers of the environment and the species of prey to avoid, but a level of curiosity rose within her. She wanted to get a close look at Mr Fox. She surveyed the splendour of his red coat, red very much like the plumage on her chest. The fox looked menacing sleek and masterful, with piercing eyes and with a sly look about him. Her eyes darted back and forth, fear rising within her.

The fox was so close, Matilda thought, but what had stopped him in his tracks? She thought she would be dead meat by now but for some reason the fox had yet to pounce but stood rigid on the spot. Matilda positioned herself and fluttered upwards whilst the fox stood at the foot of the tree looking up at her hoping to take aim at her.

"What to do?" she thought and flew around the windows which surrounded the house, hoping to find a way in to escape the fox. Luckily, the bathroom window was open, and she fluttered in and sat perched on the windowsill looking over at the tree where the fox was still positioned, looking up at the tree stalking out his intended prey, but Matilda had moved on.

"I am never going to get out," Matilda thought. "What will become of me?" she pondered. She darted around the bathroom, trying to decide what the next step would be. She had to work on an exit plan, but she was too scared to step out now in case the fox caught her and snuffed her life out.

Back at the nest it soon became apparent that Matilda was missing. Mummy Robin let out a shriek! "Where is Matilda?" she tweeted, looking around her frantically.

She counted her chicks again just in case she had miscounted. "One, two, three, …. Yes, Matilda was certainly missing," she tweeted frantically!

As she prepared to leave the nest, Mummy Robin gave strict instructions to the remainder of her brood to stay put. "Don't go anywhere," she ordered. "Stay put. I do not want anyone else going missing!"

Mummy Robin flew out of the comfort of her nest and went around to the other nesters who shared the area to inform them of her plight. Matilda's mummy knocked on the door of the starling's home.

"Hi, come in," Suzette the starling said. "How are you? Come and share this food with us," said Suzette. Suzette turned around to see a forlorn robin perched on the outside of their home. "Ooh what's wrong, you look so sad," the starling continued.

"Matilda is missing," Mummy Robin said. "She left the nest sometime this morning we think, and she has not returned."

"Really, but she is so young, why did she feel the need to go out?" Suzette said.

"If I knew the answer, I would not be looking for her, would I," Mummy Robin said frustratingly.

"Sorry," Suzette the starling said. "I will help you look for her." The two of them set out from the nest and went along the path to the nest where Larry the blue tit lived.

As they approached the nesting area of Larry the blue tit, Larry peered out from under the shrubby and noticed their anxious faces.

"What's up?" tweeted Larry.

"Matilda has gone missing," they both blurted out in unison.

"I will come and assist you. Together we will find her." Larry said.

Soon others joined the hunt for Matilda. Julie the starling, Quirky the duck, Teddy the Cocker Spaniel, Mummy Robin, and Larry the blue tit with their entire brood. It made for a peculiar sight; however, all were united in their mission to find Matilda.

Back near the old, discarded railway site, Matilda had taken a nap, loving the adventure in an absurd sort of way, oblivious to the trauma unfolding at home but also anxious to get back to her family.

She had taken refuge nesting in the broad branches of a lilac tree, the pleasant aroma enabling her to fall asleep. Perhaps upon waking she would gain some inspiration to navigate her way home and hopefully bring some food with her. She had failed in her adventure, disappointed but not to the point that this slight setback would dampen her enthusiasm to try again.

Matilda woke up suddenly, awakened from her sleep by the barking of a dog. She peered over the top of the branch and focused her gaze to where the source of the sound was coming from. She could see dog walkers on the common opposite out in the early morning sun walking their dogs. Well, they're up early, I might as well rouse myself and start the day, she thought.

One thing for sure, she was glad that the nightmare of the encounter with the fox was behind her and extremely glad to be safe from his clutches. She consoled herself on the fact that she had had a narrow escape and had been so lucky.

Up to this point, Matilda's search for food had been somewhat haphazard. Perhaps this was because she had sophisticated taste buds, or she had been looking in all the wrong places! She flew across to the riverbank for her morning paddle and spied another robin digging away at the mossy area at the edge of the riverbank.

"What was she doing?" she thought. She flew in closer to get a better look. She peered at the spot intently as the other robin tugged at a mealworm briskly and stuffed it into her mouth, the tail of the worm gliding over the tip of her beak as the robin maneuvered the mealworm into her mouth, pushing it securely to the side of her cheek. Matilda watched in awe silently, taking note of the technique employed by the robin. "Aah, so that is how it is done," Matilda chirped excitedly!

The other robin turned around on its spindly feet, almost falling over as he recognized Matilda.

"What are you doing here?" the robin tweeted anxiously.

"I went to look for food," Matilda said.

"Without Mummy or Daddy?" the other robin responded.

"Yes, I went on a little adventure, but I would like to go home with some food before I complete my journey.

Emulating the techniques Matilda had seen employed by the other robin, she franticly started digging in the grassy area, debris flying everywhere as she tugged at the mealworms pulling them out from beneath the soil! One worm, two, three, four, five, her beak was full of them. Now she was ready to fly home.

"Ready now?" the other robin chirped. Matilda nodded her head, taking care not to lose her treasure, the treasure she had worked so hard for and travelled so far to acquire.

Flying back together, they spied a strange sight in the distance, a menagerie of birds and a puppy walking around in a group. They looked at each other quizzingly and in disbelief. They swooped down to get a closer look and as they did so, Suzette the starling turned her head around and her eyes clapped on the two robins, and she let out a shriek. "Matilda, Matilda!" The rest of the party looked to see what the commotion was about. When they saw Matilda, they all resounded in their own individual verse. "Matilda, Matilda, so good to see you."

"Woof, woof," the puppy barked, joining in the chorus.

Mummy Robin scuttled over to where Matilda was standing and wrapped her wings around her, fussing over her as she did so.

Matilda's mouth was full, her cheeks bulging so much she was unable to respond, and it soon dawned on Matilda's mummy what had transpired. She had gone in search of food. She smiled to herself and mused within herself at how impatient Matilda had been, but thankful that she was home safe.

Daddy Robin returned to the nest with the food he had gathered, oblivious to the events of the day. What with the food gathered by Matilda and the food Daddy Robin had brought home, there was enough to last them for a whole week!

"What a day it has been," Mummy Robin said.

"Why?" Daddy asked.

Mummy Robin, not wanting to relive the events of the day just replied, "Well at least we have Matilda home safe and sound and good neighbours who look out for each other."

Daddy Robin smiled, still not knowing as to what his wife was talking about, but happy that she was now at rest.

Matilda, reunited with her family, embraced Daddy Robin and with the excitement of her ordeal proving too much for her, contentedly folded her wings and snuggled under the span of Daddy's wings and fell asleep.

THE END

About The Author

Jennifer Skyers also writes under her pen name,
Adina Rose Benedict and has published books across both genres, fiction, and non-fiction.

You can find other books she has written on Amazon and in a bookstore dotted around London.

Jennifer is a keen tennis player, loves travel, and can often be heard giving lectures on empowerment and purpose.

Printed in Great Britain
by Amazon